March 16, 2010

Happy Birthday

DANIEL

God bless you — love

Nanny & Taid

Tales of Heaven and Earth

Gérard Bessière has one passion: Jesus.
Priest, researcher, writer and journalist,
he explores every avenue that leads
to a better understanding of Jesus.
He is the author of several books
about Jesus Christ.

Cover design by Peter Bennett

ISBN: 1 85103 190 1

Managing editor: Jacqueline Vallon
Adviser for UK edition: Rev. David Jarmy

First published in the United Kingdom 1995
by Moonlight Publishing Ltd, 36 Stratford Road, London W8
Printed in Italy by Editoriale Libraria

Jesus Sat Down and Said...

by Gérard Bessière

Illustrated by Christine Adam,
Andrée Bienfait, Anne Bodin,
Dorothée Duntze, Georges Lemoine,
Jean-Marie Poissenot,
Dominique Thibault

Translated by Gwen Marsh

Moonlight Publishing

For Floflo, Sarah and Alexandra,
little Fleur, Anne and Laura,
Zéa and Lucie, Basile and Johnny.

One day Jesus left his village and set off down the road.

The first Jews were inhabitants of the kingdom of Judah, with Jerusalem at its centre. Later, surrounding tribes of Israelites – the people chosen by God – were also known as Jews. By the end of the 1st century AD the term was used for all belonging to the Jewish religion – Judaism. Now the term Jewish includes believers and non-believers who trace their origins to the culture made by Judaism.

He was a Jew of Palestine and his name was Jesus. He was a carpenter and joiner in Nazareth, a village dreaming among the hills. He looked a peaceful, quiet and joyful man, both gentle and strong. He seemed to be nursing a happy and important secret.

One day he tidied his tools away, swept his workshop and went out, closing the door behind him. April was smiling in the flowering bushes all along the road. The sky was an even deeper blue than usual. The ploughed fields seemed to be waiting and listening.

The name Jesus, like Joshua, comes from the Hebrew Yeshoua' which means "God saves".

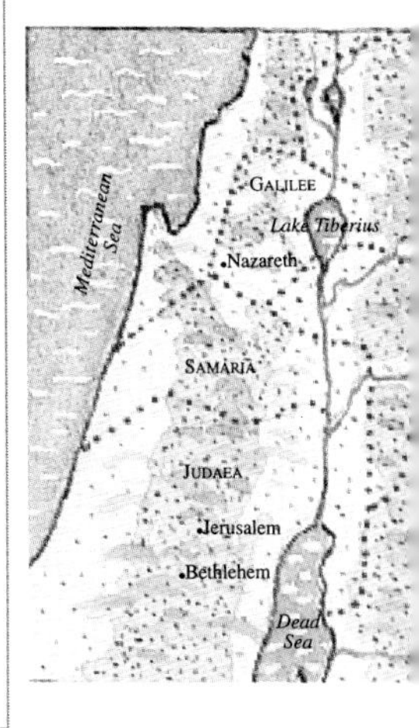

He wanted to help men to find the Kingdom of God.

Jesus will never say what the Kingdom of God is. He conveys it through word pictures and stories. He shows it by the way he lives, making it clear that it is not a political kingdom but a kingdom of peace and love.

He felt spring in his heart too. He wanted to share it with everybody, in towns and villages across the countryside. The secret message that he wanted to make known was, briefly: “What people need is a change of spirit. That is the way to thc Kingdom of God!”

People were anxious and unhappy. For a long time Israel had had no king. Foreign armies occupied the territory. People hoped that one day God himself would come and lead them. Most thought he would come as a warrior lord who would drive out foreigners and punish bad Jews, and reign over the entire world. People wondered if this would be the year of his coming.

Jesus felt the Kingdom of God germinating like a seed within him. But God, for him, was not a warrior lord. Jesus knew that God’s kingdom was something quite different. How would he tell this, first to the people of Galilee, then to all Jews, and then, one day, to everyone? How could they enter this hidden kingdom of the spirit? He would tell them stories. Perhaps that way they would understand that he was telling the story of God... and their own story.

It was commonly believed at that time that a nation’s misfortunes were divine punishment. Jews who did not observe the rules of their religion and its moral teaching were judged very severely.

From the 6th century BC Palestine was dominated in turn by the Babylonians, the Persians, the Greeks, the Egyptians, the Syrians and finally the Romans, who arrived in 63 BC.

But how could he make them realise how rich this Kingdom was?

Jesus wandered the roads of Galilee. When he came to a village, small groups of people would gather round to listen to him. He spoke of justice, equality and love between men. He spoke of God's kindness to the humblest and poorest people. His words awakened a surge of hope in the breast of each. Soon one, then two, then four, then twelve men joined him and followed him wherever he went.

One day, in a village in the midst of fields, Jesus said to them: "There was a peasant who used to go to one man's

Jesus chose the twelve apostles – meaning 'those sent' – because there were twelve tribes of Israel. This number signifies that they were sent to all the people of Israel. Their names were Simon-Peter, Andrew, James, John, Philip, Bartholomew, Matthew, Thomas, James, Jude, Simon and Judas.

Jesus compared it to this treasure that a ploughman found in a field.

Ploughs were made of wood with an iron plough-share. They were pulled by donkeys or bullocks. The ploughing just scratched the soil surface. Barley or wheat seeds were scattered by hand, then buried by piling up earth or by ploughing the land again.

farm and then another's to plough the fields. That day he was following the plough behind his donkey. It was an ordinary day. Patiently he made furrow after straight furrow. Suddenly something jarred, the plough handle jerked up and the donkey stopped. The peasant thought the plough had hit a big stone. He bent down to clear it out of the way. There was indeed a big stone: it had moved and there was a hole underneath. He scraped away the earth and saw a chest down there. When he

Or to that pearl so beautiful that one would give up all else to possess it.

Ancient eastern stories often told of hidden treasure. The storyteller showed his skill in lavish descriptions of the treasure and of all the discoverer had done with it. But Jesus doesn't say what the treasure is nor what the discoverer did with it. He captures the attention of his listeners, then leaves them to work things out for themselves.

managed to raise the lid he discovered that it was full of gold coins, jewels and precious stones. A treasure had been hidden there, doubtless at a time when foreign armies were roaming the country, pillaging everything in their path. The peasant got up quickly and looked round to see if anyone was coming: there was no-one except the donkey and a butterfly. He lifted the lid again for a moment: yes, the treasure was truly there.

He felt the rapid beating of his heart. He hurried to close the chest, replace the stone over it in the hole and cover the stone with earth. Full of joy, he left quickly with his donkey and the plough.

That same day he sold his house, furniture, garden and all he possessed and bought that field. Everybody was amazed to see him so happy. Even the donkey was glad."

And Jesus added: "The Kingdom of God is like that hidden treasure..."

Another time he told the story of a merchant who traded in pearls. He had many beautiful ones. But one morning, at another merchant's, he saw one that was truly marvellous. He couldn't sleep. He sold all his other pearls to buy the pearl that was so fine. He went off light of heart with that one pearl shining in the palm of his hand.

Jesus tells the parables of the treasure and the pearl to show the extraordinary novelty of the life he offers.

These parables are told in the gospel of Matthew, chapter 13, verses 44 to 46.

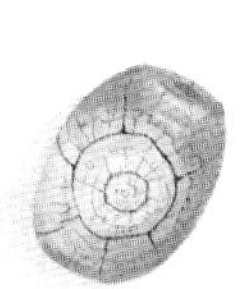

To reach the Kingdom, all you had to do was go with him.

Jesus spoke often of the paths leading to the Kingdom. One must be alert, like servants who wait up all night for their master: "When the master finds them up and ready to serve him, he will make them sit down at table and he will serve them himself."

One should not take a decision lightly: "He who wants to build a tower studies his accounts to be sure he will have the materials to finish it." In the same way, anyone who wants to enter the Kingdom must live as Jesus did. It is worth giving up everything else for it. "He who would be my friend, let him renounce everything."

Jesus compared a man who wanted to build a tower with a man who wanted to come into the Kingdom of God: in each case one must consider carefully, measure what is needed and put a price on it. This parable is found in the gospel of Luke, chapter 14, verses 28 to 33.

Parable taken from the gospel of Luke, chapter 12, verses 35 to 38.

To be a friend of Jesus means being one of his followers, living as he did and seeking the Kingdom. Christians live their life inspired by the love of God and others.

Crowds drew near Jesus to hear the amazing things he was saying...

That day Jesus and his friends were on the shore of Lake Tiberius. Fishermen's boats bobbed on the waves. People were coming from all directions to see Jesus. He had performed some miracles, healed some sick people. He said such beautiful things... People were talking about him everywhere. Many thought something extraordinary was about to happen. Some questioned him and asked him to work wonders in the name of God. The crowd pressed around him, so he climbed into a boat. From there he addressed all those people gathered on the shore.

Lake Tiberius is sometimes called a sea: the same word in Hebrew or Aramaic (yam) denotes a sea or a lake. This lake is 21 kilometres from north to south and 12 kilometres from east to west.

Jesus had cured the blind, the deaf and the dumb, lepers and those who were paralysed... but he had not worked wonders to impress the crowds. His miracles are signs: in giving a man back sight or hearing or the use of his legs he is suggesting a different kind of sight, a different hearing, a way of walking in God's ways.

He told them a story about scattering seed.

He told
them the story
of the sower: "Listen!"
he said, "A sower went forth
to sow. Some of the seed he was sowing fell by the wayside: the birds were quick to eat it all up. Other seeds fell among stones where there was very little earth. They germinated and sprouted at once but their roots were not deep. They withered in the burning sun. Others fell in thorny bushes which choked them. But some seeds fell in good soil, they grew well and tall and yielded a good harvest: thirty, sixty, a hundred times as much as what had been sown."
Jesus cried: "He who has ears, let him hear!"
A great silence fell upon the crowd of people
by the sea.

The places where the seed fell are compared with different ways in which people receive the words of Jesus. The seeds sown in a stony place are like the people who are happy to hear the message, but as soon as life becomes difficult they give up. The seeds that fall in thorns are like people too busy with daily cares and the love of money to attend to the message. The good earth is like the person who listens, and understands, and leads a better life from then on.

This parable is in the gospel of Mark, chapter 4, verses 3 to 9.

"He who has ears, let him hear!" is a way of saying: "Listen with more attention. This concerns you. Pay heed to the word that has been sown in you."

Everyone was puzzled, wondering what it meant.

Many were waiting for God to send an envoy, the Messiah, who would drive out the Romans. Israel could then be a powerful nation where justice would reign and God would be glorified.

Another day his friends were becoming impatient to know when he would become the leader of their people and change everything. He told them: "The Kingdom of God is like a man who scatters seed on the earth... Whether he's asleep or awake, whether it's day or night, the seed germinates, the stalk grows tall and the ears swell. When it is ripe the reaper comes with his scythe to harvest it."

The parables of the sower and the yeast invite the listeners to find in themselves gifts from God to be nurtured and made to mature with patience and perseverance. Gospel of Mark, chapter 4, verses 26 to 32.

Jesus wanted to make his disciples reflect on these things – they sometimes thought that their little group was rather too small to change the world: "The Kingdom of God is like a mustard seed, the tiniest of all seeds, but once sown it sprouts and grows into a plant so big that birds build their nests in its shade." And Jesus added: "God's Kingdom is like a small amount of yeast that is mixed with a large amount of flour and it all begins to rise." But Jesus' friends were anxious: they had heard that his enemies wanted to kill him. They came and told him this. He just murmured: "If the seed sown in the earth is not destroyed, it remains but a single seed. If it dies it bears much fruit..."

Gospel of Matthew, chapter 13, verse 33.

The gospel of John, ch.12, v.24.

The seed breaks apart in the ground and seems to die but a shoot is born from it and from this grows the ear of corn that is reaped.

Some people do not like seeing traditions challenged.

The word sabbath means rest. The sabbath day – our Saturday, the last day of the week – was given to God. Respect for this day was strict: no work, no going out, no activity except in urgent cases. Respect for the sabbath is still strong in Judaism.

At the time of Jesus there were people so full of their learning or their virtues that they looked down on those who were less learned, those who were poor or disabled, those who existed on the edges of society. They also despised those who did not obey every detail of religious observance, especially about resting on the sabbath, ceremonies at the Temple in Jerusalem, prayer meetings in the synagogues. In their eyes such people were sinners whom God would one day punish.

But Jesus sought out the poor and those who were

The synagogue is the house where Jews assemble for prayer and study. The word synagogue comes from the Greek and means assembly.

It was to these people that Jesus told a new story.

Jesus also told the story of a shepherd who had a flock of a hundred sheep. One day he lost one of them. What did he do? He left the rest of the flock, the ninety-nine sheep, to go in search of the lost one. He searched for a long time, then suddenly, there it was! Full of joy, he lifted the sheep on his shoulders and returned to the flock.

despised, to show that God specially loved those who were weak and rejected and that he welcomed everyone. In those times many people believed that illness was sent by God as a punishment for sin. But Jesus sought out the sick; he would actually go to them and he cured many of them. This did not please everybody – quite the opposite. The Pharisees in particular came to hate Jesus. So one day he faced these arrogant men and told this story:

"A rich farmer had two sons. One day the younger one said to his father: Give me my share of the inheritance. The father made the division of goods and lands. The son sold it all and went far away. He wasted his money. When famine came to the land, the young man found himself with nothing. He went and offered his labour to a man of property who sent him to guard his pigs. Watching them feed, he felt even more sharply the hunger that was gnawing at his stomach. He would have liked to be one of those pigs who were eating as much as they liked... He said to himself: The men who work for my father have all the bread they want while I am dying of hunger. I will go back to

The shepherd invited his friends to rejoice with him: "I have found the sheep I had lost!"

The Pharisees are Jews who know and scrupulously respect the Jewish law. They mix only with their own kind; they fear that contact with others would make them impure.

my father and say: 'Father, I have done wrong. I don't deserve to be called your son. Treat me as one of your labourers.' The next day he set off for home.

When he was still far away along the road his father saw him. His heart was full of pity. He started to run and threw himself on his son's neck, all ragged and dirty as the young man was. He hugged him in his arms. The son tried to say: 'Father, I have done wrong. I don't deserve to be called your son...' But he couldn't finish what he wanted to say, nor ask to be treated as a labourer, for his father was already calling to the servants: "Bring a robe, quickly, dress him in the best! Put a ring on his finger and sandals on his feet. Go and find the fatted calf, kill it and we'll have a feast! Look,' he cried, 'my son is here who I thought was dead but is alive again; he was lost and now is found.'

The peasants of Israel used to pick out one or more calves and keep them apart to fatten them for special occasions such as family celebrations.

The preparations for the feast began. When the older brother returned from the fields he heard music and dancing. He asked one of the servants: 'What is going on?' The man replied: 'Your brother has come home and your father has had the fatted calf killed!' The older brother was angry, refusing to enter the house. His father went out to plead with him. But he shouted: 'All my life I have done what you wished and never disobeyed you,

The return of the prodigal son as depicted in a famous painting by Rembrandt (1606-1669).

The story of the father who was generous with love and forgiveness.

Everyone thought he had gone for ever, he had broken with his father and all his family: for them it was as if he had died.

and you have never given me even a kid for me to feast with my friends. Yet when this famous son arrives who has wasted your fortune, you kill the fatted calf!' The father said to him: 'My child, you are always with me and what is mine is yours. But it calls for celebration and rejoicing when your brother – and he is your brother! – who was dead is alive again, he was lost and is found.' "

The older son represents those Jews who believe themselves to have been faithful servants of God for a long time. The younger son is a sinner. The father is God, who doesn't apportion blame and goes on loving those who turn from him.

This parable, known as The Prodigal Son, appears in Luke's gospel, chapter 11, verses 15 to 32.

Jesus was asked to dine with a Pharisee.

Neighbours and passers-by could enter a house where people were feasting. It was quite usual.

Another day Jesus was invited to dinner at the house of a man who was highly respected, one of those Pharisees full of his own merits. He arrived at the house and they sat down to dine. Neighbours and people passing by looked in on the company while they were eating and talking.

Suddenly everyone fell silent: a woman had just come in with an alabaster flask. She was well known as a woman of bad reputation. The conversation began again but everyone was

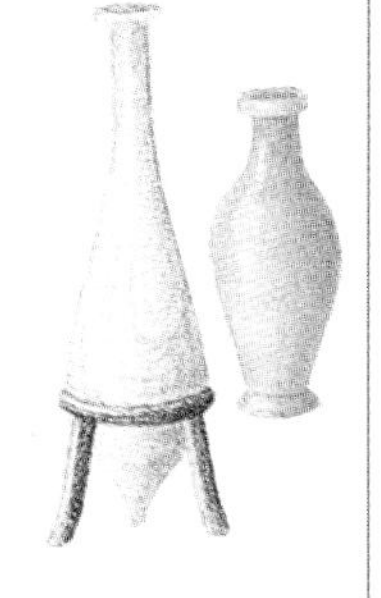

Perfume in those days was very costly. It was kept in precious flasks made of blown glass or alabaster.

At that time, in Palestine, people ate either sitting on seats or on the ground. Sometimes they reclined on divans covered in cushions.

The first gesture of hospitality when a guest arrived was to wash the dust of the roads off his feet.

watching her. She came and stood behind Jesus, who was reclining by the table as was the custom then. She knelt down and began to cry. Her tears fell on Jesus' feet. She wiped his feet with her long hair, covered them with kisses and emptied over them the perfume from the alabaster flask.

A great silence fell. No one said anything. But the highly respected host who had invited Jesus said to himself: "If this man were a prophet he would know who that woman is who is touching him, and what she does."

Jesus looked at him and said:

"Simon, I have something to tell you."

"Speak, master."

Now everyone looked at Jesus. He began to tell a story: "A rich creditor had lent money to two men. The first owed him a large amount, the second ten times less. Neither could repay the loan, so he gave it to them. Which of the two will most love the generous man?"

"I think it will be the one to whom he gave the largest

Luke's gospel does not say in what way this woman had acted badly. There is nothing to say that she was a prostitute or led an immoral life. All we know is that she was harshly judged.

Nor does the gospel give the name of the woman. Sometimes she has been identified as Mary Magdalen, but this may be incorrect.

Jesus caused a scandal by welcoming an outcast woman.

sum," Simon answered.
Jesus told him: "You are right."
Everyone at the table was paying attention: Why did he tell that story? No-one now was looking at the woman kneeling near Jesus.

So then Jesus turned towards the woman and said to the master of the house: "You see this woman? I entered this house. You did not bring water for my feet as is the custom, but she has washed them with her tears and dried them with her hair. You did not embrace me, but she has been kissing my feet ever since she arrived. I declare to you: whatever her bad deeds may be, and however many they may be, they are forgiven because she has shown so much love." And he said to the woman: "Your sins are forgiven."
The guests round the table asked themselves: "Who is this man who dares to pardon sinners?"
Jesus turned to the woman and said: "Your faith has saved you. Go in peace."

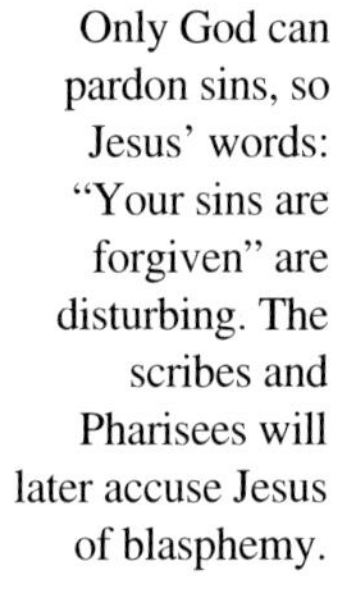

Only God can pardon sins, so Jesus' words: "Your sins are forgiven" are disturbing. The scribes and Pharisees will later accuse Jesus of blasphemy.

This parable is in the gospel of Luke, chapter 7, verses 36 to 50.

"Who is my neighbour?" a scribe asks him one day.

Jesus had come to Jerusalem, the capital of Palestine. One day a very learned man, a scribe, asked him a question:
"What must I do to have eternal life?"
Jesus asked him:
"What is written in the holy scriptures?"
"You shall love the Lord your God with all your heart and your neighbour as yourself," replied the man, then adding: "But who is my neighbour?"
Then Jesus related this story: "A man left Jerusalem, the

Scribes in Jesus' time used inkwells and a calamus (sharpened reed), but also wax tablets on which they wrote with a metal stylus.

Scribes are specialists of the Torah, the Jewish law. They belong to the Sanhedrin, an assembly which takes important decisions and has religious, administrative and legal powers.

town on the high ground, and went towards Jericho, the oasis in the valley, the town of palm trees. The road fell steeply across a barren desert where nothing grew, where there were only sand, stones and rocks. The man was descending quickly when suddenly bandits sprang from the rocks and fell upon him. He fought back but they beat him, stole his bag and wallet and made off. The traveller was left lying on the ground, stunned, unable to move. He might have been dead. Not a sound was to be heard.

Now came another man riding down to Jericho, a priest from the Temple in Jerusalem. He would surely go to the aid of the injured man! Oh no! The priest sees the man lying there, all bloody, at the edge of the road and he passes by, making a wide detour. Next came a Levite. He would help the man in his misfortune! But he doesn't! He sees the man lying quite still and he too turns away from him and rides on.

Priests and Levites were highly esteemed. Busy in the service of God, they were considered as a class apart, superior to others.

The Levites helped the priests and were occupied with Temple business.

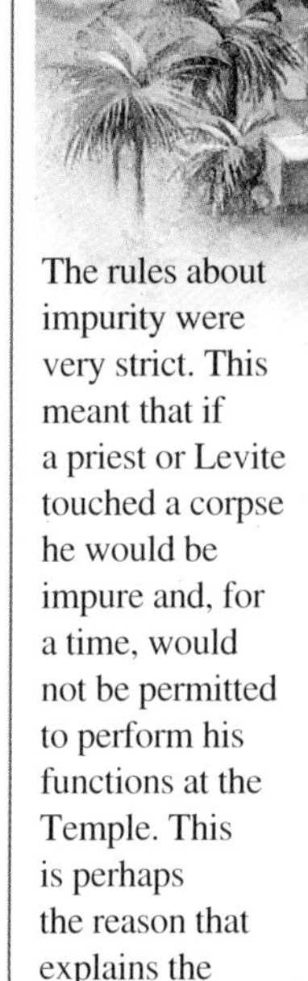

The rules about impurity were very strict. This meant that if a priest or Levite touched a corpse he would be impure and, for a time, would not be permitted to perform his functions at the Temple. This is perhaps the reason that explains the attitude of these two men who did not know if the man on the ground was still alive.

They were examples for all because they observed every detail of the Law and the traditions.

The poor injured man was still unconscious. But now there was someone else approaching. It was a man with a donkey loaded with his belongings. No hope from this one, though: he was a Samaritan, a foreigner, whom people hated. When you meet a Samaritan you keep your distance and do not greet him. That was when the unexpected happened. The Samaritan saw the injured man and came close, knelt down beside him and spoke to him gently. The man opened his eyes and stammered a few words. He was in pain. The Samaritan took care of him, dressed his wounds, lifted him up and put him on the donkey's back. Then he led him to an inn and tended him all day and all that night. The next day he had to leave so he gave the innkeeper some money and told him: 'Take good care of him. If you need to buy anything else for him I'll pay you on my way back.'"

Then Jesus asked

For hundreds of years relations between Jews and Samaritans (natives of Samaria) had been hostile. The Samaritans had built an altar to rival the Temple in Jerusalem.

Jesus told the parable of the good Samaritan.

the scribe:
"Which of the three do you think showed himself the neighbour of the man attacked by the bandits?"
"Surely the one who had been kind to him," replied the learned man. Jesus said to him: "Go, and do as he did."

The parables of the lost sheep, the prodigal son and the good Samaritan are all intended to show that God also loves sinners and to shake the arrogance of people who think themselves perfect.

A neighbour is not only one who is near but also anyone who approaches another with goodwill.

The story of the good Samaritan is in the gospel of Luke, chapter 10, verses 29 to 37.

7

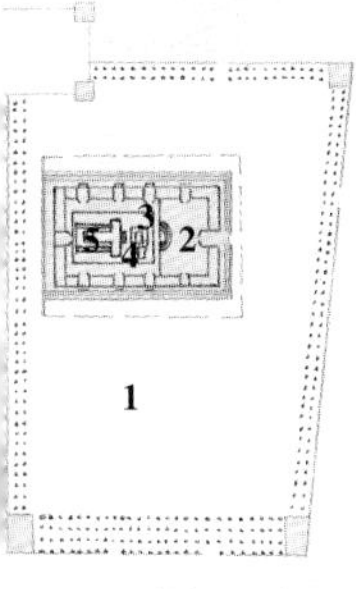

Plan of the Temple
1 - Square of the Gentiles (pagans, non-Jews).
2 - Square of the Women.
3 - Square of Israel (men).
4 - Square of the Priests.
5 - Sanctuary.

In Jerusalem the priests, scribes and Pharisees were suspicious of Jesus. They were so sure of their God, it was as if God belonged to them. Jesus, one day, told them this story of two men who wanted to go to the Temple to pray. It was a superb building, overwhelming in its enormity. As you went forward, you felt you were coming nearer to God. Ahead, at the end, was the holy of holies, a great hall, kept always closed, where God was thought to dwell.

Once past the great gates and the vast, empty, almost

The Temple had a perimeter of 1,500 metres. There were areas reserved for priests, men, women and strangers. It contained the altar where animals were sacrificed, and buildings that were considered sacred.

In the story of a Pharisee and a publican, Jesus shows...

The entrance to the sanctuary as represented on a fresco in the synagogue of Dura Europos, in what is now Syria (about AD 250).

silent courtyard the two men entered the Temple. They came from different sides; they didn't know each other. One overtook the other and went right in. That was the Pharisee. Standing very upright, he began to pray: "My God, I thank you that I am not like other people, thieves, wicked and vile, and especially not like that man behind who is not honest... As for me, I fast twice a week and I give away a tenth of what I earn." The second man remained near the back. He was a man with a shabby reputation. This was the publican, or tax collector. He didn't dare go further forward. He saw the Pharisee, far in front, his head held high, looking so worthy... He himself was bowed, as if his weight was a burden to him. He didn't even dare to raise his eyes. He beat his breast and started murmuring: "My God, have pity on me, sinner that I am!" And he kept repeating the same words: "My God, have pity on me, sinner that I am."

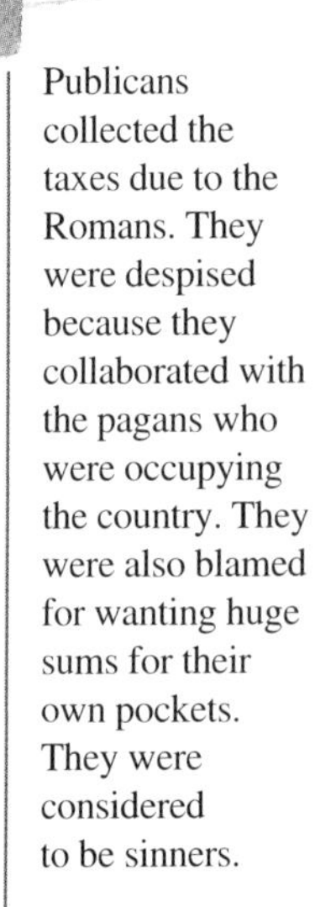

Publicans collected the taxes due to the Romans. They were despised because they collaborated with the pagans who were occupying the country. They were also blamed for wanting huge sums for their own pockets. They were considered to be sinners.

A coin minted in the year 42-43 of the Christian era.

...that a sinner can be worth more than a proud man.

The Pharisee and the publican, from a Byzantine painting of the 12th century.

Jesus stopped for a moment, then he asked: "Which of these two men pleased God and returned home the better for his prayers? It is the second, the one who didn't dare to push forward and who asked for pity."

And he concluded with the words: "Anyone who sets themselves up above others shall be cast down, but those who humble themselves shall be raised up."

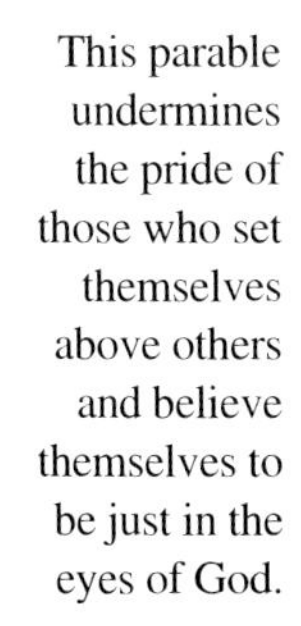

This parable undermines the pride of those who set themselves above others and believe themselves to be just in the eyes of God.

It is from the gospel of Luke, chapter 18, verses 9 to 14.

Jesus knows that many wish for his death. One last story explains...

Jesus had unmasked the murderous plans of his enemies when he told in their presence the story of the wine-growers who beat and kill their master's servants, In the end they kill his son too, so as to get the vineyard for themselves.

When Jesus understood that his enemies were seeking him out, to arrest him and put him to death, he told one more story; it was to be the last.

"When the Son of man returns on the last day all the nations will be gathered before him. He will say to them: 'Come, you whom my Father has blest, the Kingdom prepared for you since the beginning of the world is yours. When I was hungry you fed me, when I was thirsty you gave me a drink, when I arrived as a stranger you took me in, when I was ill you came to see me, when

...that he will stay among men, especially among the poor and humble.

This parable is told in the gospel of Matthew, chapter 25, verses 31 to 41.

I was in prison you visited me...'
The people will say to him: 'But when did we give you food and drink, when did we take you in or visit you?'
And he will reply: 'Whenever you have done these things for anyone, for the humblest and most needy, you have done it for me.'"

Jesus was arrested. They made a show of judging him. He was condemned to death and crucified. But soon his friends discovered that he was alive again and they proclaimed this news to all – that he was alive in God, in themselves, in the faces of all those who are in need...

And they still hear his voice in the stories he used to tell, the parables that they cherished in their hearts like a treasure, a pearl, like a seed or yeast... like an invitation to go forth and tell a wonderful message of love.

Palestine at the time of Jesus

The Philistines, originally from the shores of the Aegean Sea or Anatolia, invaded Egypt towards 1175 BC. They were driven back and settled on the coast of Gaza. The Greeks gave the name of this region, Philistia, to the whole country from the Mediterranean to the valley of the Jordan, so it became known as Palestine.

Jesus was born and lived in Palestine. The name Palestine comes from the Philistines who were masters there for a long time. The territory corresponds roughly to the Israel of today.

A little country between the sea and the desert

About 200 kilometres from north to south, and 50 to 100 from west to east, Palestine was surrounded by deserts.
From west to east – there are rich coastal plains; a mountainous region; the deep valley through which the Jordan flows from Lake Tiberius to the Dead Sea; the hills of Transjordan – 1,200 metres at their highest.
From north to south the country has three regions: Galilee, with both Jews and non-Jews, open to trade and peoples from other lands; Samaria, with a mixed population from the time of the Assyrian invasion of the 8th century BC; and Judaea, with the city of Jerusalem – the heart of the nation with about 30,000 inhabitants.

The population

The population in Jesus' time, mainly Jewish, was about 600,000. Many people lived by growing wheat, barley, vines, figs and olives and kept sheep and goats. Others were potters, carpenters, cabinet-makers or workers in metal and leather.
Alongside the landowners and rich merchants there were casual workers employed by the day or for a harvest season. There were many also who were without work, who were ill or disabled.

Left: a model of Jerusalem in the first century.
1 - The Temple
2 - The palace of Herod.

Crockery and an oil lamp in terracotta from the 1st century discovered in Jerusalem.

Flour, wine and oil were made in mills worked by men or donkeys (left-hand margin).

Top of page: Bas-relief from the Arch of Titus, commemorating his victory in Palestine. After the destruction and looting of the Temple of Jerusalem, Titus' troops brought the great seven-branched candelabra back to Rome.

Political and religious life

Roman centurion of the occupying army in Palestine At his belt he carries a sword and a dagger and he holds a pilum (a sort of short javelin). His shield is made of layers of wood covered in leather.

Rome, the occupying power

From 63 BC the Romans occupied Palestine. They put Herod on the throne in Jerusalem, and he reigned from 37 to 4 BC. He was known as Herod the Great. He was an efficient ruler: he undertook to rebuild the Temple of Jerusalem to be sure of peace with the Jews; he created the port of Caesarea, encouraged trade and made the cities safer. But he was a cruel man.

After his death his kingdom was divided between his sons. Archelaus reigned over Judaea and Samaria, Herod Antipas over Galilee. In AD 6 the Emperor Augustus deposed and exiled Archelaus. From then, a series of Roman governors ruled. One of these, Pontius Pilate, who held office from AD 26 to 36, had Jesus put to death. Pilate lived at Caesarea on the coast and came up to Jerusalem for the Jewish feasts.

Social life

Rome imposed taxes on Palestine. Natives of the country were appointed to collect the taxes: these men were called publicans. They were looked down on by the Jews.

The Roman army, infantry and cavalry, stationed in Palestine or on the frontiers, numbered about 3,000.

The Romans left in place the various structures by which Jewish society in Palestine was ordered. There was a Grand Council known as the Sanhedrin in Jerusalem, the Temple's own police, and the tribunals in the towns and villages which were also called sanhedrins.

Herod had many fortresses built, including, in about 20 BC, a fortified, circular palace on a hill near Jerusalem. It was called the Herodion.

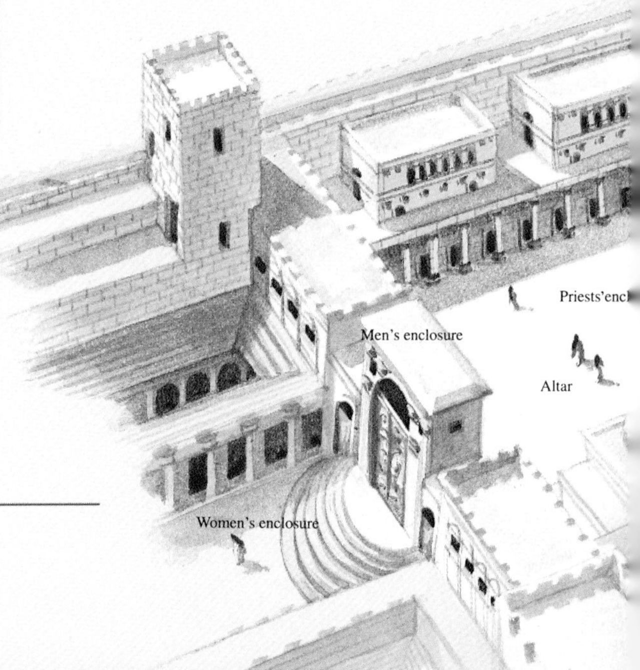

Centre page: a High Priest and a Levite. The former wears twelve precious stones on his chest, symbols of the twelve tribes of Israel.

The Temple of Jerusalem, for Jews, is where God dwells, and therefore the most holy place of all. Within one vast courtyard are strictly reserved areas where non-Jews are not allowed.

At the heart of life: the religious person

In the middle of these pages you can see the Temple of Jerusalem to which all Jews looked, whether they lived in Palestine (about 600,000 people) or abroad (6 to 7 million). The great feasts were celebrated at this Temple, and the people brought animals for sacrifice.

Powerful clergy

The High Priest, appointed or dismissed by the king or governor, was close to political power. He was very rich. He was surrounded by 7,200 priests forming 24 teams who shared the duties of offering sacrifices, and 9,600 Levites also in 24 teams who were responsible for music, and for policing the Temple.

Holy of holies

Holy

The scribes, guardians of the Law

The Law, contained in the Bible or the Tradition of the Elders, was interpreted and passed on by scribes. Their long training led to ordination at about 40. Highly respected, they taught in schools attended by many Jews, and also presided at tribunals, particularly at the Sanhedrin.

Synagogues

There were also synagogues, especially in towns and villages further from the Temple. The synagogues were houses where people gathered to study the Bible and pray. The head of the synagogue was elected by the Elders. The most important assembly was the one on the Sabbath. There were prayers, a reading in Hebrew of a passage from the Law and a text from a prophet. These readings were then translated into Aramaic, the language spoken by the people, and were commented on. The ceremony ended with a blessing.

Different religious groups

Many groups existed close to the official religion: Pharisees, pious and demanding; Sadducees, rich and conservative; Essenes, who lived in monastic communities in the desert; Baptists, who placed more importance on immersion in water than on the Law or sacrifices in the Temple; Zealots, who led the armed struggle against the Romans. All of them, in their own ways, were waiting for the reign of God.

Among the Baptists, the most famous is John (above, painted by L and J Salimbeni, 15th century). John foretells the coming of Jesus and will baptise him in the Jordan.

Below: a coin showing the façade of the Temple.

Left:
12th-century Catalan nativity.

Who is Jesus?

AD stands for anno domini, Latin for Year of our Lord, from which the Christian era is counted. Jesus was born between 4 and 7 years before this era. When he was about thirty he left Nazareth, and travelled to other villages and towns. He announced that the Kingdom of God would come soon. He called upon his fellow countrymen to adopt a new way of life in order to prepare for the Kingdom of God. He cured the sick and those possessed of devils, and performed miracles as signs of the Kingdom to come.

A messiah awaited

Many were expecting this Kingdom and God's envoy – the Messiah – who would bring news of it. They believed that God would give Israel back her political power and drive out the Romans. They also believed God would punish 'sinners' – those Jews who failed to follow the rules of their religion. They were expecting spectacular events. But Jesus fled when they wanted to make him king.

He refused to perform wonders. He appealed to the consciences of those who came to him. He had striking new ideas: "Blessed are the poor, the meek, those thirsting for what is right; blessed are the peace makers..."

He called on people to wake up and be free, to undergo a deep change of heart. It was essential, he said, to love God and other people.

He showed this in his own conduct. He was free of the barriers of the society in which he lived. It was a society where lepers were kept apart, for sickness was thought to be God's punishment for sin; there were some jobs that were despised, and women did not have the same rights as men...

Messiah comes from the Aramaic word mesiha meaning anointed. The word was used of those who were smeared with holy oil for a function conferred by God – kings and priests. After the 1st century the term is reserved for God's envoy who is awaited. The Greek word for messiah is Christ.

Some dates:
BC 20 to 10: Rebuilding of the Temple of Jerusalem.
Between 7 and 4 BC: Birth of Jesus.
4 BC: Death of Herod, last king of Palestine.
AD 1: Invention in Rome of windows of frosted glass.
AD 9: Romans defeated in Germany.
AD 25: Buddhism spreads in China
AD 26: Pontius Pilate governor in Judaea.
About AD 30: Jesus crucified.
AD 122-6: Hadrian's Wall built.

Jesus flouts rules: here he meets the Samaritan woman (from a fresco in a Roman catacomb)

In Israel lepers lived apart from society. They dressed in rags and had to warn people from distance of their approach. They could form groups to help each other. The term leper was also used to include people ith skin diseases that could be cured.

The people of Israel always remembered the :liances God had made with their ancestors and particularly the one made on Mount Sinai when Moses received the Ten Commandments. These set out ules for a way of life faithful to that alliance.

An attitude that shocked

Jesus felt free to behave as he wished. He disregarded rules that separated people. By mixing with sick people, touching lepers, talking with women and having them among his closest disciples, Jesus shocked many strict Jews. They believed that God loved only those who were 'perfect'. Jesus wanted to show that God offered love and pardon to all, and first to those rejected by others. He shared meals with people of bad reputation, he welcomed sinners, he wanted people to live as brothers and sisters. He told them to call God "Our Father".

A danger to the social order

Jesus soon had opponents and even enemies. Many of the men in power, among the educated and the priests, saw Jesus as a danger to society, morality, religion and the future of the nation.
The conflict intensified. When Jesus caused a scandal at the Temple by driving away the merchants selling animals for sacrifice, his enemies decided to arrest him. They brought him to judgment and had him put to death. He was crucified in the year AD 30. But soon his disciples were declaring that he was alive again, and they set out to tell the world what they had seen and heard.

How do we know about Jesus?

Jesus' message is known to us thanks to the four gospels of Matthew, Mark, Luke and John, and the Acts of the Apostles, Epistles (letters) by Paul, Peter, John, James and Jude, and the Apocalypse. These writings date in their finished edition from the years AD 60 to 95. They form what Christians call The New Testament. This is distinct from The Old Testament which tells of the alliances the God of Israel made with his people before Jesus Christ.

Top of page: The lamb (Jesus) surrounded by the emblems of the four gospel writers. (From a 9th-century book of gospels.) Matthew's emblem is a man, Mark's is a lion, Luke's is an ox, and John's is an eagle.

Top centre: Jesus (on the left), from a 13th-century stained glass window.

The art of the parable

The word parable is of Greek origin and means comparison. It's a story or a description through which another meaning is suggested. It helps the listener to reflect and to grow in understanding.

Jesus illustrated everything he did with short tales called parables.

Both simple and subtle

Parables don't give ready-made answers, they provoke listeners to think for themselves. Parables set the scene of the tale in Jesus' own time and always tell of some action, for they aim to bring about a change in the listener. A parable conveys its meaning through the whole story: it makes a point.

A strategy for involving the listener

Hearing the parable of the two debtors, the Pharisee who had invited Jesus to dinner states his position. It is not until the end of the story that he realises that it's about himself. Rather than risk making people angry by condemning their attitudes, Jesus told a story that left his listeners free to form their own opinions.

The parable lets you pursue the logic of a situation to its limit. But it avoids giving offence to people at the start, and perhaps blocking discussion.

A note of exaggeration

Thus, making a great fuss of the return

Centre-page: a parable illustrated in the Echternach Gospel (10th century): a king gives a banquet for his son's betrothal but his guests all have good reasons not to come. So the king invites beggars and disabled people and feasts with them. In the same way everyone is invited to the Kingdom of God but many exclude themselves.

of the prodigal who has wasted his heritage, or risking the life of one's own son when the vineyard workers have already killed the servants, etc. – this element of exaggeration is meant to confuse the listener. Then he can more readily question his own values and understand the different morals of the Kingdom of God.

Parables are also found in the Holy Scriptures of the Jews well before the time of Jesus and in the texts of rabbis in the first century and after.

In the parable illustrated below (from the 10th century Gospel of Echternach) Jesus is foretelling his own death. A man entrusts his vineyard to some wine-growers. But when he wants the return from the harvest due to him and sends, successively, three servants to collect it, each is beaten or killed. Finally the man sends his son and he too is killed.

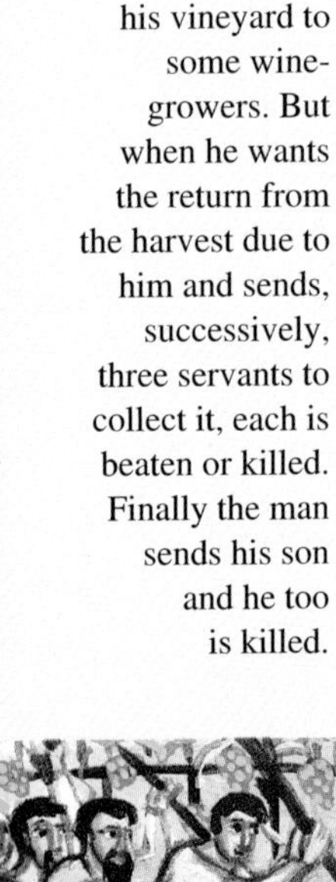

Top of page: the apostle Peter (right) and Paul, the founders of the Christian Church (4th-century bas-relief).

A religion is born

Centre page: a representation of Christ from a 6th-century Egyptian icon.

At first Jesus was portrayed as the Good Shepherd (3rd century). In the 4th century Jesus appeared with another face (above).

From the 4th century onwards many oil lamps bear the chrisma: the two first letters of the word Christ interlaced.

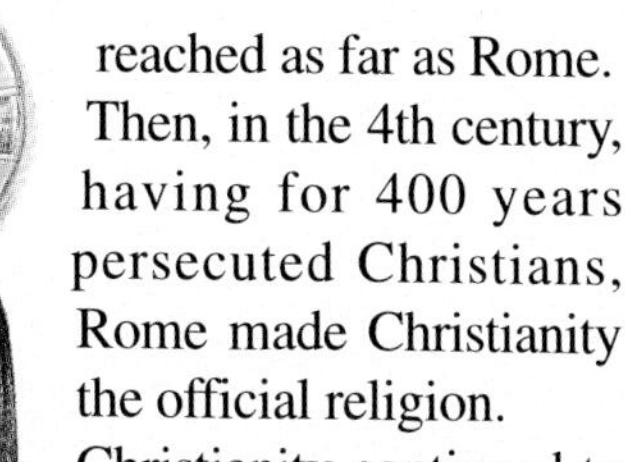

Jesus left no writings. But he left chosen men, disciples. At first they stayed in Jerusalem, inviting other Jews to join their community and take up their way of life. They prayed at the Temple and had not yet broken with Jewish tradition.

But Jesus' followers were persecuted – many of them went to found communities elsewhere. They came to be known as Christians.

Paul, a former persecutor of Jesus' disciples, was converted in the year AD 37 on the road to Damascus. Thanks to him, non-Jews joined Jesus' followers and were admitted to the churches. Paul was an active preacher in Asia Minor, Greece and Rome, where he was beheaded in AD 64. He left many letters to the communities he had founded.

The Good News – that is what Gospel means – thus reached as far as Rome. Then, in the 4th century, having for 400 years persecuted Christians, Rome made Christianity the official religion.

Christianity continued to spread across Europe, Asia, Africa and later to America and Australia.

Churches took different approaches, sometimes splitting from each other. Today there are many Christian churches, including the Roman Catholic Church, the Orthodox Churches, Protestant and Reformed Churches, the Anglican Church and various sects and movements, all based on the teachings of Jesus.

Christianity in today's world.

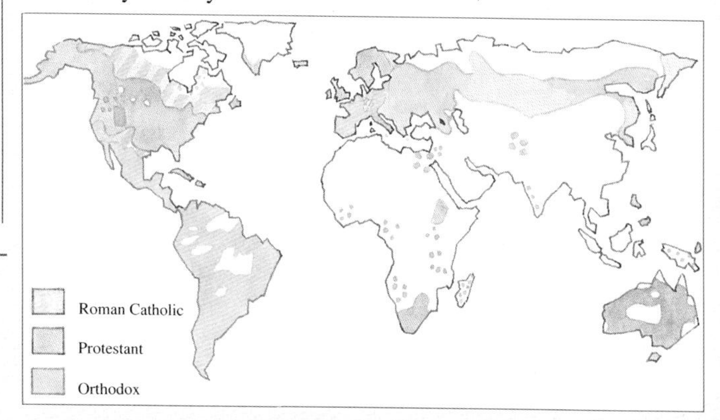

Some dates:

AD 65 -95: Gospels written.

AD 70: Destruction of the Temple at Jerusalem.

From AD 92: Persecution of Christians.

AD 313: Emperor Constantine is converted.

AD 325: Council of Nicaea formulates the faith of the Church in the Nicene Creed.

AD 800: Charlemagne emperor.

1054: Split between Roman and Eastern Churches.

1492: Discovery of America.

1520: The Reformation separates Roman Catholics and Protestants.

19th century: Christian missionaries active throughout the world.

Look out for other titles in this series:

SARAH, WHO LOVED LAUGHING
A TALE FROM THE BIBLE

THE SECRETS OF KAIDARA
AN ANIMIST TALE FROM AFRICA

I WANT TO TALK TO GOD
A TALE FROM ISLAM

THE RIVER GODDESS
A TALE FROM HINDUISM

CHILDREN OF THE MOON
YANOMAMI LEGENDS

I'LL TELL YOU A STORY
TALES FROM JUDAISM

THE PRINCE WHO BECAME A BEGGAR
A BUDDHIST TALE